Effective
Delegation Skills

(A Practical Workbook to Help You
Master the Art of Delegation)

CW01426006

Gerard Assey

Effective Delegation Skills
By
Gerard Assey
© Copyright 2022 by Author

Publishing Agency:
Collection Skills
19/18, Palli Arasan Street
Anna Nagar East
Chennai - 600 102

E-Book ISBN No: 978-93-92492-07-5

Paperback ISBN No: 979-82-15559-93-2

Contents

List of Illustrations in the Book
Preface
Objectives of this Book: What will this Book help you Achieve?
Why People do not Delegate
Barriers to Delegating- by Manager, Subordinate and Organization
Why Delegate?
Benefits of Delegation
What to Delegate
Who to Delegate to? Identifying the Right Person
When to Delegate?
What should not be Delegated?
Support and Resources
Achieving the Balance: Under/ Over Delegation
Understanding Levels of Control- Responsibility and Authority
Key Principles of Delegation
Practical Steps to Delegate Successfully
Monitoring with Appropriate Feedback
Tools to Monitor the Delegated Task
Reviewing the Delegation Process
Conclusion
About the Author

List of Illustrations

1. Most common reasons for not delegating
2. Deciding on a Task
3. Selecting the Right Person for the Task
4. Indentifying Tasks your Subordinate could do
5. Delegated Tasks Checklist
6. Delegation Chart- to track work
7. Providing Positive & Constructive Feedback
8. Monitoring Tools

Preface

One of the most difficult areas of a supervisor's job (especially for newly appointed supervisors) is that of delegation and one of the fundamental problems that people have when taking the step up to management is their inability to delegate effectively. New managers often struggle with this, but even more seasoned leaders can default, as one of the most difficult transitions for leaders to make is the shift from doing to leading. Therefore one of the most important skills that a manager can master is learning how to delegate, for the more one progresses up through the levels of management, this skill becomes increasingly important, enhancing ones productivity to great extents.

Contrary to popular belief among many, being a leader does not mean you must do every task to ensure it is done properly. Being a leader includes empowering others to improve the overall organization, as well as providing the necessary tools to optimize the performance of the group. Empowering typically comes through delegating responsibilities to others. As more members get involved (and take ownership of projects and assignments) the more effective the organization will become.

Delegating has been shown to improve work efficiency and benefit the organization in ways that may not be obvious initially. In the long term however, delegating empowers the team, builds trust, motivates and allows for new and innovative ideas, which in turn leads to the development of the team members' creative and decision-making skills. Real and thoughtful delegation, with support, is a great way to actually stretch and develop people, and this is often more powerful than through periodic professional development. For leaders, it helps you learn how to identify who is best suited to handle tasks or projects, for at its best, delegation is empowering people to do the work they are best suited to. It allows them to invest themselves more in the work and develop their own skills and abilities. It also allows the manager to do other important work that might be more strategic or of higher-level.

A study by Harvard Business Review determined that delegating can actually increase organizations' income and overall efficiency. Not only does delegation empower others in the organization, but it also helps optimize the performance of the overall group. The better you are at delegation, the more successful you and your team will be. The difference between success and failure is often a matter of distancing yourself from a task and delegating.

Thus good delegation **saves time, develops people, grooms a successor, and motivates.** On the other hand, poor delegation will cause you frustration, de-motivates and confuses the other person, fails to achieve the task or purpose itself and can even cripple organizations.

By the very nature of the job, a supervisor is responsible for more than he or she personally does. They must therefore learn the art of delegating work to others. However, deciding on the nature and number of tasks to be delegated can cause considerable difficulty. A supervisor's overall responsibility can be thought of as having two areas:

An "area of supervisory tasks", and an "area of delegation"

The area of supervisory tasks represents all those tasks which a supervisor rarely delegates, whilst the area of delegation represents tasks which can be delegated.

The area of delegation represents tasks which may be done by both the supervisor and the team.

It is all about giving others the authority to act on your behalf, accompanied with responsibility and accountability for results. A leader cannot do all of the work for an organization; if one tries, he or she will not be successful at leading. Most leaders have some difficulty delegating responsibility. Most often they would prefer to do the task themselves to make sure the "job gets done right." While this method can be more expedient, it can also breed apathy among non-involved, unmotivated members eventually resulting in the loss of members. Sharing your authority with others can be the greatest single motivator in retaining members and strengthening the organization.

To successfully delegate, managers should consider the nature of the task, communicate openly and ensure their subordinates understand their intentions, expectations and needs- especially if their team is working remotely.

As can be seen, effective delegation is therefore one of the most valuable yet difficult skills a manager can master, as successful delegation certainly takes time and effort, but the benefit it gives is enormous and invaluable.

The best part however, is that this skill can be learnt and this is what this little book will help you do. In addition to reducing your workload it enhances the abilities of your staff. Delegating tasks and responsibilities to your employees enables them to handle more complex assignments and allows you to advance within the organization.

This Book will hopefully provide a practical guide to boosting your own and your team's productivity through the successful art of delegation.

Exercise:
Before you get deeper into the subject, think about this skill: Delegation, your experience of delegation or delegation that you have observed at work. Then write down in a few lines what you think it means:

Objectives of this Book: What will this Book help you Achieve?

This Book will immensely help explain:
- ✓ Why delegation is an important management tool.
- ✓ Why delegation is one of the most important management skills you can master.
- ✓ How to achieve a balance in the extent to which you delegate
- ✓ How to decide whether or not a task is suitable for delegation.
- ✓ How to use the step by step process of delegation to delegate effectively and control your team more efficiently.
- ✓ The key rules of successful delegation that will motivate and empower your team.
- ✓ How to accurately monitor delegated tasks and avoid the over-reporting trap
- ✓ Different ways to delegate tasks and how to provide effective instructions to produce better results
- ✓ Common delegation pitfalls and how to avoid them
- ✓ Techniques for giving effective feedback
- ✓ How to get a job done by someone else effectively and efficiently.
- ✓ With delegation, your staff will have the authority to react to situations without referring back to you

Exercise
List the various objectives you have in mind (for you/ your organization/ others) by you reading this book?
1.
2.
3.
4.
5.
6.
7.
8.

Why People do not Delegate

Here are some key reasons:
- ✓ Unable / Unwilling to let go
- ✓ Lack of faith and confidence in others
- ✓ Fear that subordinates will perform better than them- insecure feeling
- ✓ They can't trust anyone else to do the same quality job.
- ✓ Believing that they alone could do quicker or better
- ✓ They feel no one has their ability, and that they are the only ones capable of performing the task.
- ✓ Lack of training in delegating
- ✓ They are too busy
- ✓ They would feel guilty passing on their work.
- ✓ People feel that asking somebody else to do something implies that they are not able to do it themselves and are not really up to the mark
- ✓ The delegate's success may indicate that they be lacking competency.
- ✓ In an attempt to protect their position of authority, some people like to keep resources, especially information to themselves. An obsession with control
- ✓ A desire for the limelight
- ✓ They are ineffective teachers and cannot develop others
- ✓ They view a reduction in their work load as a threat to their ego or self worth.
- ✓ They are overly attached to a habit or routine.
- ✓ Fear that someone else might do it better than them and that will embarrass them or expose their incompetence.

- ✓ They don't have time to train people. It's just easier to do it by themselves
- ✓ May avoid delegating due to resentment at others being given credit for the successful completion of the task- Allows jealousy to stand in the way

Most Common Reasons for NOT Delegating

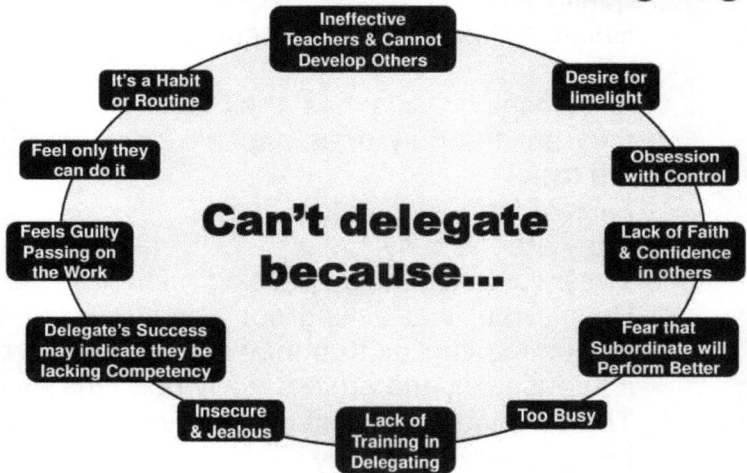

Can't delegate because...

- Ineffective Teachers & Cannot Develop Others
- It's a Habit or Routine
- Desire for limelight
- Feel only they can do it
- Obsession with Control
- Feels Guilty Passing on the Work
- Lack of Faith & Confidence in others
- Delegate's Success may indicate they be lacking Competency
- Fear that Subordinate will Perform Better
- Insecure & Jealous
- Lack of Training in Delegating
- Too Busy

Barriers to Delegating- by Manager, Subordinate and Organization

Some of the barriers to delegation related to the Supervisor or Manager are:-
- ✓ Insecurity
- ✓ Wanting to do everything personally
- ✓ Retention of power
- ✓ Unwillingness to delegate authority
- ✓ Lack of confidence in subordinates
- ✓ Unwillingness to set standards of control
- ✓ Unfamiliarity with how to delegate
- ✓ Desire to make identity or be in the limelight
- ✓ Tradition and norm of organization
- ✓ The inability to assume the managers role
- ✓ Fear of competition
- ✓ Acceptance of the Indispensable person theory

Some of the barriers to delegation related to the Subordinate are:
- ✓ Fear of making mistakes
- ✓ Lack of the right incentives
- ✓ No access to resources
- ✓ Lack of confidence
- ✓ Convenience
- ✓ Dependence on managers and others for every decision
- ✓ Inadequate information
- ✓ Excessive workload
- ✓ Not enough motivation

Some of the barriers to delegation related to the Organization are
- ✓ Size of the organization
- ✓ No precedent of delegation
- ✓ Degree of centralization or decentralization
- ✓ Inadequate or lack of proper planning
- ✓ Defective organization structure
- ✓ Splintered authority
- ✓ Lack of unity of command
- ✓ Ineffective control techniques
- ✓ Non-availability or Incompetent managers
- ✓ Environmental influences

Exercise
From your experience what are the key reasons why people do not delegate?
1.
2.
3.
4.
5.

Barriers to delegating related to Subordinates:
1.
2.
3.
4.
5.

Barriers to delegating related to the Organization:
1.
2.
3.
4.
5.

Why Delegate?

At first the answer seems obvious: "You can't do everything yourself".
This is one very good reason; but there are many others. Such as:
- ✓ To even out workloads of others
- ✓ To allow for planning activities
- ✓ To add variety to a repetitive workload
- ✓ To give training or coaching opportunities
- ✓ For the development and growth of the team/ succession planning.
- ✓ Provides you with the opportunity to develop your team members by increasing their morale and motivation and develop the workplace competencies of subordinates.
- ✓ When you delegate some chores, as a manager you will have more time to plan, to organize, and to motivate
- ✓ Delegating encourages creativity and innovation
- ✓ Delegation reveals the capabilities and shortcomings of subordinates. You will never really know what your people are capable of, if you do not allow challenging new assignments their way
- ✓ As a supervisor, it will make you a much sought after leader
- ✓ As a manager it frees you up to work on the bigger assignments and picture
- ✓ When you develop your skills as a manager by delegating, you give yourself more time to work on your other skills and capacities, which could earlier not have been drawn out.

- ✓ You will become more efficient as the stress will be less, which means that your vision will be wider.
- ✓ The team and subordinates will feel satisfied and content, which will increase their loyalty and lower the chances of them looking for jobs outside the company.
- ✓ Delegation gives you time and energy to do more important and larger tasks

Benefits of Delegation

The difference between success and failure is often a matter of distancing yourself from a task and delegating. Here are some key benefits:
- ✓ Higher efficiency
- ✓ Increased motivation
- ✓ Develops the skills of your team
- ✓ Better distribution of work through the group
- ✓ Makes the manager focus on more important tasks
- ✓ Preparing the "second line"
- ✓ Enables team leaders to: develop a committed and motivated team
- ✓ Helps to boost team moral, improve efficiency and productivity, and promotes enthusiasm, innovation, and cooperation - all of which are vital to a company's bottom line
- ✓ It stimulates creativity and develops and encourages innovation in your team
- ✓ Helps draw on the expertise of team members
- ✓ Helps make better decisions
- ✓ Helps make effective use of time
- ✓ Helps team members get a variety of experience by increasing their opportunities to participate
- ✓ Gives members a feeling that they are trusted and valued members of the team, which encourages greater commitment and loyalty
- ✓ It helps create learning opportunities that improve retention
- ✓ It helps increase their knowledge about the organization and the work of the team as a whole. It increases the flow of information at

all levels, and effective communications throughout an organization are essential for good decision-making.

✓ It allows managers and leaders to focus on key areas of planning and organizing

✓ Enables you to maximize your success since, instead of wasting time on administrative tasks and low-value projects; you can now focus on the strategic activities that require your expertise and authority.

✓ By delegating, it provides management to assess their team's advancement and promotion potential

✓ It helps improve management/ subordinate or team relationships and bonding with employees

Exercise

What according to you are the Key Reasons why you should delegate? What are those specific benefits to you/ your team/ organization when you delegate?

1.
2.
3.
4.
5.
6.
7.
8.
9.
10.

Benefits to You:
1.
2.
3.
4.
5.

Benefits to the Team:
1.
2.
3.
4.
5.

Benefits to the Organization:
1.
2.
3.
4.
5.

What to Delegate

What should I delegate?
One of the most difficult decisions to make, especially for newly appointed supervisors, is just how much or what specific area of work is to be delegated.

You would first of all need to decide if the said task needs to be delegated in the first place. Do you want to give it away? Do you enjoy it or feel it is so important that true delegation will not take place? Be true to yourself and delegate those tasks which ought to be handed over. In other words, you should always concentrate your energies on those parts of your work that are the most advantageous to the organization and its development.

The Eisenhower Technique is a simple decision-making tool that can help you decide what to do with each task in front of you. It is said that when he wasn't invading North Africa, France and Germany, Dwight Eisenhower, the 34th President of USA, was best known for being a legendary decision maker and he put together a matrix by which it can help separate our actions. There are essentially four types of work that land on our desk:

Quadrant 1: Urgent and important (tasks you should do immediately).

Quadrant 2: Important, but not urgent (tasks you should schedule to do later).

Quadrant 3: Urgent, but not important (tasks you will delegate to someone else).

Quadrant 4: Neither urgent nor important (tasks that you will stop doing).

See Illustration provided below:

Deciding on a Task

| | **Urgency** | |
| High | | Low |

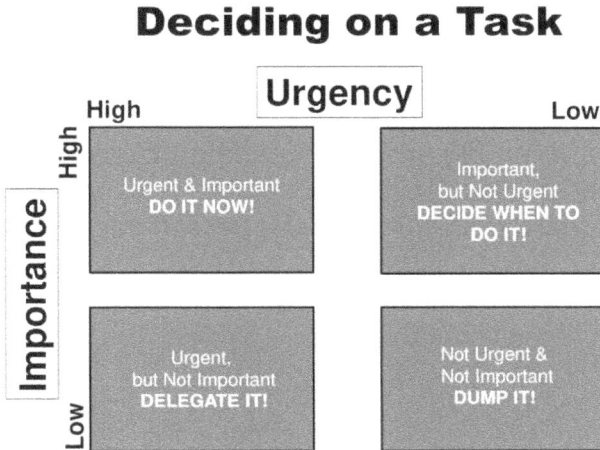

Here are a few areas you would like to keep in mind on what to delegate:
- ✓ Routine Jobs- together with power to make decisions
- ✓ Whole Jobs- gives a sense of achievement
- ✓ Jobs that others can do better than you or by more cost effective ways

And some of those jobs which are suitable for delegating may include the following:
- ✓ Jobs which individual team members can do as well as or better than you; Jobs for which team members are specifically competent
- ✓ Jobs which serve to develop individuals; Developmental jobs
- ✓ Jobs which are of low to medium priority; Medium to low priority jobs

- ✓ Jobs which are routine; Routine jobs
- ✓ Jobs which appeal to individual team members and they get a sense of achievement and enjoy the same; Attractive jobs

Here are some Questions you might like to consider before assigning any task:

- ✓ You must ensure that the person you delegate to, knows what you want-the desired outcome? What results do you expect the employee to deliver?
- ✓ The person concerned understands how to do the task? Understands how the task fits into the larger picture. How does the assignment contribute to larger goals of the department or organization?
- ✓ Key details- What essential details should you communicate?
- ✓ Has he/ she been given sufficient authority and resources to succeed? Resource support may include any of the following? A budget? Other helping hands (e.g., tech support, someone to type/ photocopy) Materials or machine time? Training etc. What other material resources or support do you plan to provide or would they need?
- ✓ Is motivated to do a good job? Formally accepts responsibility. Authority- How will you make sure the employee has the authority to succeed at the task?
- ✓ Deadline and checkpoints. Do you have a deadline in mind? What are the logical points at which you would check progress?

- ✓ How would this assignment help the individual overall in his/ her development?
- ✓ Do you have everything in place to ensure their smooth take-over of the assignment?

You might like to initiate a dialogue by asking a few questions to ensure all is understood:

- ✓ Are you comfortable handling this? How do you feel about taking on this assignment? Am I asking for more than you can handle right now?
- ✓ What problems do you foresee? How do you plan to handle them?
- ✓ Is coming Tuesday a reasonable deadline to expect this to be completed?
- ✓ Do you have any further ideas/ suggestions on how to improve this even better?
- ✓ What would you do if_____ happened?
- ✓ What all would you need to ensure you complete this successfully?

Exercise

In your role as a Manager, what are parts of your job that you would delegate to someone else (and why would you do so), and which ones would you carry out yourself?

Delegate to Others:

1.
2.
3.
4.
5.
6.
7.
8.

Do by Myself:
1.
2.
3.
4.
5.
6.
7.
8.

Who to Delegate to? Identifying the Right Person

When deciding or choosing the Right Person for the job, it is important to try to give members tasks that they can do best or are interested in. If members are truly not interested or motivated in working on a task, they might not do a good job. Their motivation will be much higher when they know that they are trusted by you as their leader.

When identifying the Right Person to delegate the job to, there are few questions you would need to ask:

- ✓ Who will find the job challenging and/or interesting? Who will benefit from taking on the job?
- ✓ What experience, expertise, skills and attitudes are needed to do this job? Keep in mind KASH of the person you are delegating to (the knowledge, attitude, skills, and habits).
- ✓ Who has carried out a similar job before? Who do you think has the necessary skills, but has not yet used them for a job like this?
- ✓ How well does the person understand the context of the assignment?
- ✓ How much training or coaching, if any, will be required?
- ✓ To what degree is the assignment aligned with the person's workplace goals or interests?
- ✓ Is there someone who would regard doing the job as a form of recognition and/or reward?
- ✓ How urgent is the job? If you need the job done urgently, you will have less time to spend briefing and supporting an

inexperienced team member. You may want to delegate an urgent job to someone who has done a similar task before, and who is already competent to do it.

✓ What are the consequences of missing deadlines, or making mistakes? By thinking about the importance of getting the job right first time and the deadline for completing it, you can judge the level of risk you are prepared to take in giving the task to someone who has never done it before.

✓ What is the most economical way of getting the job done?

✓ Would the person's other work obligations suffer because of this assignment?

✓ Finally, to avoid a disappointing outcome, you must delegate to a person who has the following characteristics: Time available? Interest in the task? Capability and reliability? Closeness to the problem or issue? Potential to benefit from the assignment

Selecting the Right Person for the Task

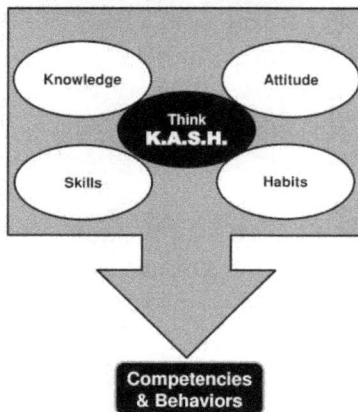

Knowledge

Attitude

Think
K.A.S.H.

Skills

Habits

Competencies
& Behaviors

Note: As and when you identify specific expertise, interest or skills in your team you could make a note of it for future. You could do a similar exercise as shown in the illustration below to identify potential and assign tasks:

Identifying Tasks your Subordinate could do

Subordinate	Tasks I can Delegate	Potentiality of Subordinate	Remarks
1. Sarah Philip	Prepare and Present to the Marketing Team the New Product Development Process on 30th Sept	1. Has the K.A.S.H. Yes __ No __ 2. Has Expertise Yes __ No __ 3. Is Capable Yes __ No __ 4. Is Dependable Yes __ No __ 5. Is Interested Yes __ No __ 6. Would benefit Yes __ No __ *(This is only an example. You can add your own criteria)*	
2. Name Two			
3. Name Three			

When to Delegate?

DO DELEGATE when:
- ✓ There is a lot of work.
- ✓ When you feel someone else has a particular skill or qualification that would suit a task.
- ✓ When someone expresses an interest in a task.
- ✓ When you think a particular member might benefit from the responsibility (i.e., an emerging/ potential leader in your organization)

As a manager, you would always need to keep the bigger picture in mind of what your organizations' objectives are. Before delegating any task, there are a few factors you might like to consider first.

You can do this by asking yourself 'If I delegate this task':
- ✓ Will it give me more time to focus on tasks that are of greater value to the organization?
- ✓ Will it allow me to develop the skills of my team member by expanding their capacity/ expertise and experience in this area?
- ✓ Will it offer someone with a fresh view of the task the chance to provide a more innovative solution than I would have done?
- ✓ Will this be in the interest of all? (Or am I being self-centered?)

If the answer to any of these questions is 'yes,' then you should consider delegating the task.

As an initial step it is best and safe to delegate:
- ✓ Routine tasks.
- ✓ Planned tasks.

✓ Tasks that a team member has expressed an interest and enjoys doing so.

✓ Tasks that the individual has some expertise in But remember, that you must be mindful not to always delegate unpleasant tasks as this will not develop or motivate your staff, but can be misconstrued as a punishment- rather than developing or helping them move forward.

Delegated Tasks Checklist

Task to Delegate	Key Details	Expected Outcome	Deadline	Possible Volunteer	Skills Needed	Resources/ Support	Authority	Check Points

What should not be Delegated?

It is also important to understand when you should NOT delegate. You should resist the temptation to pass on tasks that have been delegated to you, as it is crucial to be able to control issues that arise and ensure they are resolved between you and the task owner. Delegation should also not be used as a strategy to handle last-minute tasks. The nature of such a task does not provide sufficient time for you to control the risks involved or to provide a sound brief.

So here are a few guidelines on what NOT to delegate:

DON'T DELEGATE:

- ✓ Your own extremely important matter with serious consequences, emergencies, matters of exception to a policy, etc.
- ✓ Things that are usually your specified responsibility
- ✓ Things you would not be willing to do yourself.
- ✓ A task to a member who may not possess the skills necessary to do the task successfully
- ✓ Work which is of a confidential nature.
- ✓ Tasks for which you do not have the authority in the first place.
- ✓ Your company regulations and policies may specify jobs which only you can do, or there may be procedures which only you can undertake.

Your answers will depend on your own circumstances, but here are some examples of work activities that you would not delegate: disciplinary action; counseling staff; reviewing the performance of team members; your role in promoting health and safety at work; planning and organizing the work activities of the whole team

Exercise

In your role as a Manager, what are some of the tasks you would refrain from delegating? Why?

1.
2.
3.
4.
5.
6.
7.
8.

Support and Resources

As a Manager, when delegating, it is important that you give the team/ individual all the necessary support and resources to carry out the task, besides the given authority.

Think of 5M's when planning this:

Men: The people that can help the individual. What training would be required? Who will provide the same? Any additional manpower required?

Machine: Any equipment/ gadgets/ tools that can help speed the process?

Money: Has sufficient funds been allocated?

Material: What more information will be required? Who will provide or from where to obtain? What were past trends when handling this same type of task or assignment?

Method: What will be the process? Is the individual familiar with the same?

Exercise:

For an upcoming task or project, think of all the Resources/ Support you/ your subordinate may require and list the same:

Resources Needed   By Whom? How & When?

1.
2.
3.
4.
5.
6.
7.
8.

Achieving the Balance: Under/ Over Delegation

Under-Delegation

Under-delegation is when one does not pass down responsibility to the team or others below, and tries to do everything by oneself instead. By enabling the subordinate to participate in deciding what is to be done, helps the manager to make better decisions. It also helps to build up a good team spirit and develop individuals.

Under-delegation is not giving sufficient authority and responsibility to those who work for you; by not using the team's expertise in decision-making, and can often result in managers doing too much themselves; resulting in being overworked. They consider it less bother to do the job themselves or they have too much concern for their own reputation; or they lack confidence in their team's ability; or they feel insecure in their job as a manager; or are just too keen to do the operational job themselves.

Here are some main reasons listed…

- ✓ Lack of time for delegating
- ✓ Lack of confidence in the ability of team members: Treat team members as incompetent and do everything for them.
- ✓ Fear of losing their reputation by sharing their workload: Managers who hesitate to delegate often do so because they believe it will enhance their own reputation if they do the job themselves.
- ✓ Easier to do the work themselves than to delegate it- it is quicker, rather than explain to the subordinate

- ✓ A feeling that they can do the job better than any member of their staff
- ✓ Feeling Insecure- Insecure managers fear that passing on part of their job to someone else means that they will no longer be needed themselves

The effects of under-delegation can include: a feeling of 'them' and 'us' among the team; the manager feels overworked and is not able to give time to managing the team; team members cannot actively participate; resulting in a lack of team spirit among the team.

Effects of Under Delegation on the Supervisor/ Manager who delegates too little are:
- ✓ Is overworked
- ✓ Has no time for planning
- ✓ Makes no provision for work being done in his absence
- ✓ Is taken advantage of by the team
- ✓ Has not developed his team
- ✓ Will not have a work-life balance
- ✓ Will stress out soon
- ✓ Will not be able to grow and take on more
- ✓ Will never make a great manager

Effects of Under Delegation on the Team/ Individual when the Supervisor/ Manager delegates too little are:
- ✓ Individuals don't develop
- ✓ Motivation is low
- ✓ Team becomes complacent
- ✓ Team feels insecure
- ✓ Teams become too lazy and dependant

- ✓ Can make the talented restless, resulting in attrition

The Reasons for Under- Delegation
Unacceptable reasons would include that the Supervisor/Manager:
- ✓ Does too much making the team lazy
- ✓ Unwilling to share with others on what to do
- ✓ Is unsure how a task is done, so covers up by not allowing others to become involved
- ✓ Is insecure and sees others as threat to their position.

Some acceptable reasons would be
- ✓ High workload: Where a particularly heavy schedule puts pressure on the team, and the supervisor or manager helps out.
- ✓ Keeping in touch: Where a supervisor or manager involves him/herself in tasks normally undertaken by others, but now does it/ gets into it occasionally, only in order to keep in touch with the team's activities.

Exercise
What according to you are the Effects and Reasons for Under-Delegation?
1.
2.
3.
4.
5.
6.
7.
8.

What is one sign that a manager is delegating too little?

Over-Delegation
Over-delegation on the other hand is when too much responsibility is delegated- when a manager passes on responsibility to others and does not control the task that has been delegated. It may be that the managers are trying to avoid their responsibilities but they must realize that when something goes wrong, the subordinate member delegated to make a decision will quickly pass on any blame straight back to the manager - where it belongs. And this is not good and can lead to serious conflicts.
Managers over-delegate because they lack experience in the job or they are poorly motivated to do their job; or they could be afraid of making errors themselves. The level of direct control the manager takes in delegating is related to the amount of trust they have that the person who will carry out the delegated task will do a good job. And this can be developed by going carefully through the process of delegation and helping the team member to be successful by using an appropriate level of control

The effects of over-delegation can include: the manager loses control of the team; the authority of the manager is undermined; resulting in little unity in the team and disrespect for the manager.

Effects of Over-Delegation on the Supervisor/ Manager who delegates too much are:
  ✓ Causes resentment
  ✓ Loses respect and credibility
  ✓ Loses touch and maybe loses control

✓ Denotes incompetence of manager

Effects of Over-Delegation on the Team/ Individual when the Supervisor/ Manager delegates too much are:
- ✓ Team is overworked and inefficient
- ✓ Team is prone to making mistakes
- ✓ The team can feel that the manager is taking advantage of them
- ✓ Team resents the leader
- ✓ Rise in conflicts and misunderstanding
- ✓ Staff turnover is high

The Reasons for Over- Delegation
Unacceptable reasons would include that the supervisor:
- ✓ Dislikes the task
- ✓ Is too lazy to do the task
- ✓ Delegates to prove authority
- ✓ Thinks everything should be delegated
- ✓ Is unable/ does not know how to do the task

Some acceptable reasons would be:
- ✓ Training/ Coaching: where the tasks are normally done by the supervisor, but is delegated as part of a training session for development of the individual or team
- ✓ Succession planning: where an individual has been identified for potential promotion or on deputization in the absence of the supervisor, certain tasks may be delegated which would normally be done by the supervisor.

Exercise

What according to you are the Effects and Reasons for Under-Delegation?

1.
2.
3.
4.
5.
6.
7.
8.

Exercise:

1. What is one sign that a manager is over-delegating?

2. Think about the managers you know, or have known, at your workplace and the ways in which they have delegated jobs to members of their team. Which category did they fall into?

Understanding Levels of Control-Responsibility and Authority

Very often the newly promoted manager may not be clear with the difference between their own roles and responsibilities and that of their team's, other than maybe having a different job title; by having the feeling in them that all do the same work!

It is important therefore for the manager to be able to identify the assignments between the team and themselves, as one can only delegate authority, but never responsibility.

When the manager delegates effectively, he/ she is in overall control, and the manager, based on the following factors can decide on the level of control:

- ✓ The requirements of the job/task
- ✓ The preferred approach
- ✓ The knowledge, skills, abilities, experience and attitude of the individual or team;
- ✓ The motivation, commitment and interest in the work by the individual
- ✓ Periodic/ Timely feedback
- ✓ And most importantly is the TRUST factor! The extent to which the manager trusts the individual to do a good job
- ✓ Finally, remember that you, as the manager, retain overall responsibility for a job you have delegated.

Various Types and Levels of Delegation

There are various types of 'Delegation of Authority'- basically four different types of delegation of authority that you will see prevalent in organizations.

And each type of delegation of authority is based on different factors and they are:

- ✓ General or Specific Delegation: This is based on the job assigned.
- ✓ Formal or Informal Delegation: Based on the process of giving authority.
- ✓ Top to Bottom or Bottom to Top Delegation: This is based on the hierarchy.
- ✓ Lateral Delegation: It requires a group or team to work in parallel

When delegating a job or assignment, an important element of doing so is assessing each task being delegated and grading it according to the amount of authority that it requires on the part of the individual who will be performing it.

And for this, ideally you could think of doing it through 4 basic levels:

Level 1- Where Zero Authority is needed

Level 2- With Minimal Authority

Level 3- With Moderate Authority

Level 4- With Total Authority

Remember however that for each assignment requires a different amount of delegation. This means taking into account both the needs of the assignment and the abilities, skills, and other factors listed above of the person.

Taking the approach of gradually increasing the delegation level as time goes by can greatly benefit your employees. Not only will they become more confident in taking the initiative in tasks, but it will make them more useful to you later on down the line.

For a manager starting out, it would be best by seeing it through these 7 levels or steps of

Delegation and when to use each of them, especially for key decision areas:

1. Telling: This level is usually when the subordinate is relatively new to a task. You make the decision and show how to do it explaining the motivation. This is more the 'do as I say'!

2. Selling: This is for someone a little more experienced than the one above. In this case, you make the decision by enabling them understand the benefits, and reason behind them doing it and that you made the right choice. Here you help them feel involved.

3. Participating: As they grow in their experience and expertise on the job, you can now ask for their inputs first, which you may like to take it into consideration before making a decision- that respects their opinions.

4. Agreeing: At this stage, you might like to enter into a discussion with everyone or the individual involved, and reach consensus about the decision. This is a joint decision.

5. Advising: In this case, it will be solely their decision, but you may offer your opinion and advice, hoping they listen to your suggestions

6. Enquiring: You first leave it to the others to decide, and afterwards, you may ask them to convince you of the wisdom of their decision.

7. Delegating: This is the final stage, wherein you have total confidence in the team/ individual and therefore leave the entire decision to them and you don't even want to know about details. This is the final level of delegation. It is also the **most extreme** form and is the **highest level** of delegation. It provides the one being delegated to with the most amount of

control and empowerment but also the most amount of accountability.

Key Principles of Delegation

Before we understand some key principles of delegation of authority, let's look at what 'delegating authority' means in the first place. Simply put, it is the process of sharing responsibility with others and trusting them to fulfill a set of objectives for a particular assignment. Delegation of responsibility can be very effective once we understand how to delegate properly. And a good thumb rule would be to best follow the 6 'Rights of Delegation'

- ✓ The right task/assignment
- ✓ The right circumstance/ situation
- ✓ The right person
- ✓ The right leader
- ✓ The right direction/communication
- ✓ The right tools/ resources/ support

Here are some key Principles of delegation that you can keep in mind before you consider delegating any task:

1. Principle of Functional Definition: Whenever delegating any assignment, there should be clarity regarding the tasks to complete, the methods of performance and the expected results, with the goals, objectives and targets clearly defined. Before delegating powers to the subordinate, the manager should be able to clearly define the goals as well as results expected from them, along with the standards of performance.

2. Principle of Unity of Command: According to this principle, every individual in the organization should be solely accountable to another person. This ensures a sense of personal responsibility because

that individual is ultimately answerable to someone. Although it's possible for someone to be accountable to multiple people, it's best to avoid that as it can create complications and conflict.

Principle of Delegation by Results Expected: This principle is to ensure that the degree of authority delegated to an individual manager be adequate enough to assure their ability to accomplish the results expected of them. And this must be effectively communicated to all concerned. Without this level of authority, they will be unable to complete the task, as others they need to interact with, will hinder their progress due to lack of 'real' authority.

Principle of Absolute Responsibility: This says that the authority can be delegated but responsibility cannot be delegated by a manager to his subordinates, which means responsibility is fixed. It must be noted that the responsibility for the activities of subordinates, who have been assigned duties, remain at all times with whoever originally delegated the task. By delegating, it does not mean that the manager can escape from his/her responsibility. He/she will always remain responsible till the completion of task.

Principle of Parity of Authority and Responsibility: According to this principle, the manager should keep a balance between authority and responsibility. Both of them should go hand in hand. The degree of authority that is delegated in conjunction with the task has to be consistent with the level of responsibility and role of the subordinate. If someone is given the responsibility to carry out a task, then that person must be given enough independence to carry out the task effectively. On the other hand, the subordinate should not be given so much authority that they may abuse the position. The authority should be given in such a way which matches the task given to him/her. Therefore, there should be no degree of disparity between the two.

Principle of Authority level: This principle suggests that a manager should exercise his/her authority within the jurisdiction/framework given to him/ her. It emphasizes on the degree of authority that is well-defined and the level up to which it has to be maintained. Moreover, one can't delegate authority unless that person is clear about the scope of their own authority. To avoid any overlaps, there should be a clear indication of everybody's roles.

Principle of Scalar: The scalar principle emphasizes the need for a chain of direct authority and command of relationships throughout the organization. It helps to understand where everyone stands in the organization in relation to one another. This helps in ensuring effective communication in the organization because information has to flow in the decided order. Knowing this also helps people quickly reach out to the right person in case of any emergencies. This principle is especially useful in places with flat organizational structures, where hierarchy isn't very prominent.

Principle of Positive Motivation: When an individual is motivated through rewards and recognition, he/ she is certain to push harder and perform better. This process is called 'positive reinforcement', and works effectively with the right type of incentives so that members are motivated to take responsibility willingly. A simple act of acknowledging a person's efforts can make a big difference.

Practical Steps to Delegate Successfully

1. Decide what to delegate: You must first know what it is that you plan to delegate. Not everything can be delegated. Some work is strategic or business critical, and would benefit from your personal attention. Before you begin delegating work, evaluate the importance of the work and the implications of delegating it. Confirm in your mind that the task is suitable to be delegated. Does it meet the criteria for delegating?
2. Prepare: Make sure to prepare the task before delegating it to someone. An employee will never achieve great results unless the correct preparations have been made beforehand. Take enough time and care to lay the groundwork.
3. Identify a suitable person for the task: Keep in mind KASH of the person you are delegating to (the knowledge, attitude, skills, and habits). Make sure that the person you are delegating a job to is capable and competent enough for the task. What are your reasons for delegating to this person or team? What are they going to get out of it? What are you going to get out of it? How will it help them, you and the organization? When deciding who you should delegate too, ask yourself these questions:
Do they have the time to take on additional work?
Do they have the skills to complete the work

accurately?

Does the work make sense for their level of expertise?

4. Delegate an entire assignment to a single person: A big mistake that inexperienced leaders make is to split a job between multiple team members. This does nothing but add confusion and complication where it is unnecessary, and can even de-motivate individuals as they will not have a feeling of accomplishment. If several people become involved in performing different aspects of the task, it becomes difficult for individuals to see where their individual responsibilities begin and end. This results in elements of the task potentially being duplicated or left unperformed as individuals think it is someone else's responsibility. Even if a team will work on the task, make sure to delegate the job to one team member.

5. Explain the task clearly. Set clear goals: It is up to you to provide your team with all the relevant information necessary to complete the task and a clear end-goal for them to aim towards. Include this in the brief. Ensure that your Goal or Objective has the 'SMARTER' ingredients when you cover them. Think SMARTER for Success!

    S-Specific
    M-Measurable
    A-Attainable
    R-Realistic
    T-Timely
    E-Ethical
    R-Ready: Get, Set, Go!!!

6. Set realistic deadlines: When briefing the member to whom you have delegated, the deadline must clearly be mentioned along with the reason for that timeframe. Enquire if this would be ok for them.

7. Confirm that the member understands completely: Never assume that the team member completely understands what you instructing them to do. While you think you may be clear, you never know what gets lost in communication. Confirm that they understand everything before leaving them to get on with the task. It takes only a few seconds but can save huge amounts of time and confusion in the long run.

8. Communicate your trust in their ability and do it often enough.

9. Get the member's commitment: This is another part of the delegation process that is easily skipped over. Make sure that the team member has accepted the task before leaving them to it. Many times a manager has assumed the team member has taken the task, only to find that it is not complete later on because they could not accept it. Think of it as a relay race- make sure you've handed the baton to the next runner before letting go.

10. Leave room for ingenuity / initiative/ creativity of the individual

11. Grant the necessary authority to do the job properly: It is impossible for your subordinate to complete a project or activity if they do not have the required authority to do so. When you delegate authority, it is your responsibility

to notify all of the interested parties that you have done so.

12. Provide the necessary resources, backup and support whenever needed.
13. Focus on the results, not on the process.
14. Keep in touch with the person for support and monitor progress. Review periodically but do not get too close: Make sure that you receive regular progress reports. It is okay to intervene if a task is overdue, or if you hear that work is not progressing as it should. The key to effective delegation is, knowing when to be involved and when not to be.
15. Provide constructive and positive feedback: Make sure that you are giving feedback on the individuals work periodically. Employees must know that they are on the right track. Don't forget to offer advice and encouragement if they need it.
16. Evaluate Performance
17. Praise / Give due credit/ Acknowledge a job well done: Everyone needs praise. Don't forget to congratulate or thank the employee when they complete a task well. It can go a long way and it will set a precedent for others wanting to take on more.
18. Learn from every task delegated: What can you improve on in future to better your skills in this area?

Exercise

Having made it this far in your knowledge on Delegating, outline what 'Practical Steps you will undertake to Delegate Successfully' from now. Let this be your master list, by building up on it every time you learn something new:

1.
2.
3.
4.
5.
6.
7.
8.
9.
10.
11.
12.
13.
14.
15.
16.
17.
18.

In the Illustration given below, is a simple chart to help you keep track of the work you are delegating:

Delegation Chart

Task/ Project	Delegated to	Deadline	Follow-up	Completed	Remarks

Monitoring with Appropriate Feedback

Once tasks are delegated, employees need appropriate monitoring and periodic constructive feedback on their job performance. It is vital that you not only monitor progress, but also provide regular feedback to the team member. Giving constructive feedback is not easy, and telling someone they've made a mistake or didn't meet expectations is tricky. The words you use and how you say them matter a lot. Instead of getting angry or letting mistakes slide, provide constructive feedback that helps your employees perform better next time. First and foremost, constructive criticism needs to be positive, objective, specific, actionable, and timely. So here are some tips on how to carry out a positive feedback session:

1. Ensure the employee is comfortable and at ease. They must know, you are there to help them

2. Be Positive: Sometimes constructive feedback can be misconstrued as negative criticism, so keeping a positive tone is the key. A common way to do this is to "sandwich" a critique between two positive comments. For example, if you are providing feedback to your employee about a report, you might tell the person that the quality of work and level of details are excellent, but that he/she could improve the next report by adding a few more visuals. Then finish by thanking them for the job and saying that you look forward to seeing her next report more appealing.

3. Be Specific: Specific information about how the job was performed is more meaningful than comments such as "Thanks for doing a good job" or "You need to do better". Specific feedback tells a team member what behavior you want them to continue and/or what behavior is unacceptable.
4. Be Timely: Give feedback while there is still time to act upon it.
5. At the Appropriate Place: Be aware of appropriate times and places to give feedback. Follow the old adage, "praise in public and criticize in private". If you need to discuss inconsistent job performance or failure to complete job tasks, then set up a private meeting with the employee.
6. Never give Feedback when you are Angry. You will need to be calm, thinking about solving the problem and moving forward.
7. Focus on Solving and Helping out with the Issue, and not get into Blaming: State what went wrong. Explain how you want them to improve. Reinforce what success looks
8. Be Empathetic: Be sensitive to what the individual is going through. Try to be sensitive to the timing of feedback if employees are going through a difficult time period. This is not to say that managers should avoid giving feedback but rather that they should convey empathy if employees are struggling with personal issues and be prepared to offer support such as employee assistance programs.
9. Focus on behavior, not the person: Feedback given to employees needs to always focus on

the behavior of the team member not on intangibles such as their attitude or intention. We cannot measure, quantify or see an employee's attitude or intention. But we can witness behavior and actions. Rather than telling an employee they need to have a better attitude or that they need to be nicer to clients, tell them specifically what words or actions demonstrate their poor attitude or poor job performance. When you focus your feedback on specific behavior and actions, employees will know what they need to do differently as well as what they need to continue doing well.

10. Ask for Employee's Feedback: As an expression of humility and openness, ask your people for their feedback on your delegation methods. Can your style be better? Did they feel that you were helpful? Did they feel comfortable with you?

11. Work on providing ongoing coaching in areas specifically needed

12. End on a positive note: Feedback is also a major contributor to motivation and empowers people by enabling them to build upon their successes and lets them know that their efforts are appreciated. So work on keeping their morale high at all times.

13. Thank the Employee for undertaking to complete the Task: Research shows that there is a strong correlation between employee performance and how appreciated they feel. Without them tackling your tedious tasks, you wouldn't have nearly as much time to focus on the strategic activities that drive your success.

Providing Constructive & Positive Feedback

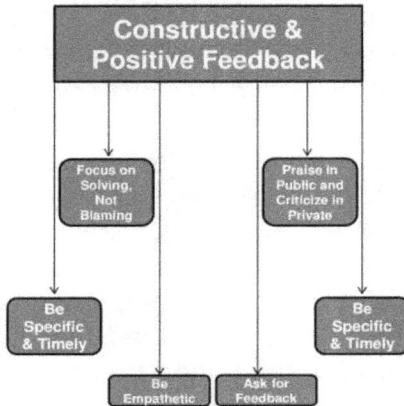

Exercise

Once you have delegated a task, what steps would you adopt to monitor and provide appropriate feedback to ensure the objectives are met

1.
2.
3.
4.
5.
6.
7.
8.
9.
10.

Tools to Monitor the Delegated Task

There are many ways that you as a Manager could monitor the delegated task. One way to ensure that you as their manager knows what is happening on an on-going basis and have a hold, rather than be caught by surprise, is to make sure that you use a variety of tools as part of your monitoring. The most popular tools are:

Monitoring Tools

Emails

Video-Conference

Reports

On line Software & Apps

Periodic Meetings

Sitting in Review Sessions

Informal Chats

Exercise
What other methods or tools can you think of to add to the above list?
1.
2.
3.
4.
5.

Reviewing the Delegation Process

Delegating a task is, of course, only half the job. You must follow up with an evaluation of the person's performance- both for your benefit and for his/her benefit. So the last step in a delegation process is your responsibility. You need to check how the delegated task was performed. Should you make some changes to increase productivity in the future? The final debriefing consists of a two-way discussion about how the delegated task went. Will you need to make some adjustments to the workflow and/or the way you delegate in future? Here are some steps you can adopt:

- ✓ Thank the member for the efforts and commitment towards the job.
- ✓ Set a time for evaluation of performance
- ✓ Keep lines of communication open- Have an open mind
- ✓ Was he/she the right person for the task delegated?
- ✓ Have the employee reflect on their own performance on the task or project.
- ✓ Ask questions, such as what they thought went well, what they thought could have been better about the project, and what they would do differently if they could do it again.
- ✓ Were they clear on the goals/ objectives of the assignment? Did they have clarity?
- ✓ Were the deadlines realistic?
- ✓ Did they have a complete understanding of the task and the outcome desired?
- ✓ Did they have complete control and authority?

- ✓ Did you give them sufficient freedom to complete the task in their preferred way?
- ✓ Were the necessary resources made available when required?
- ✓ Were they provided with sufficient support from you? Were you there when required?
- ✓ Have them provide feedback on your performance as a delegator. Specific questions can be helpful: 'Where could I have been clearer? What other types of support would have been helpful to you'?
- ✓ Did they have genuine interest and motivation, or did they feel forced into it?
- ✓ Were you as the manager happy with the periodic reporting? How can this be better?
- ✓ Provide feedback to them on how you think they did?
- ✓ On a 1 to 5 scale, how would you rate your own Delegating Skills?
- ✓ What could you do from the next time to improve this score?

Exercise
Having completed the task now, what steps would you put in place to ensure follow up with an evaluation of the person's performance- both for your benefit and for his/her benefit.

1.
2.
3.
4.
5.
6.
7.
8.

Conclusion

I hope this book has been of immense benefit to you and your team and has provided you with a better understanding of the role that delegation can play in the success of your business.

As you have noticed by now, delegation helps us to avoid overloading your shoulders and prevents burnout. It's a way of reducing work for you. You are delegating the responsibility to someone else so you can focus on something else- the more important and bigger things. Delegation lets you save time, money, and energy, so you can use that time, money, and energy to pursue what you love and other important issues, enabling both you and the subordinate to grow.

Remember that the process of delegation is just like any other leadership exercise. You need to start with a strategy, communicate it effectively, and celebrate your team's successes. If you do that, you'll be able to reap the huge benefits of delegation without sacrificing morale.

As the noted Management Guru- John C Maxwell says: *"If you want to do a few small things right, do them yourself. If you want to do great things and make a big impact, learn to delegate"*.

So in closing, let me just leave you with this thought: Sometimes, letting go is the best thing you can do. And, delegation can prove to be beneficial for you, your team and the organization as a whole.

So Get Ready, Set, and Let Go!

About the Author
'GERARD ASSEY'

Gerard Assey is a Graduate in Economics, a PGD in Management (HRD) and holds a Doctorate in Leadership. Gerard holds several International Qualifications in Sales, Debt Collection, Training & Teaching, and is a 'Fellow' of the prestigious 'Institute of Sales & Marketing Management'-UK, a Certified NLP Practitioner, a 'Certified Trainer', an 'Accredited Management Teacher-Behavioral Sciences', a 'Certified Competency Facilitator', a 'Certified Management Consultant'- (the International credentials of a professional management consultant, awarded in accordance with global standards of the ICMCI); and a Certification from the University of Michigan in 'Successful Negotiation: Essential Strategies and Skills'
He is also a Member of the 'National Association of Sales Professionals' backed with several years experience in varied industries, both in India and Overseas. He also holds an 'Etiquette Consultant' Certification from the USA (by Sue Fox, Author of Best Seller: 'Business Etiquette for Dummies'. She has trained some of the top celebrities' world over). He was also a recipient of a scholarship for extensive training in Japan on 'Corporate Management for India'.
Gerard Assey is 'Founder & Chief Corporate Trainer' of the Group: '**Citius, Altius, Fortius Unlimited**'- an

organization that **celebrated 20 years of Glorious Service** in 2021, focusing on 3 Core Competencies: **People. Performance. Profit**; in functional areas of Sales & Marketing, HR & Organizational Development, covering Recruitment, Training & Consultancy!

Having managed organizations with large Sales Forces in India & Overseas, his specialization cover extensive areas of Sales Training (All levels - Presentation, Negotiation, Key/ Strategic Accounts Management & Managerial Skills for all sectors), Bid Proposal/ Capture Planning/ Management Trainings, Retail Sales, Customer Service & Customer Retention Programs, Training for Prevention & Collection of Debt, Self & Personal Development Programs (Time Management, Teamwork & Team Building, Business Etiquette & Personal Grooming, Leadership & Managerial Skills, People Management Skills, Train-the-Trainer etc), including preparation of Custom-designed Business Manuals for Internal (HR, Induction, and Sales etc) & External use (Instruction, User Manuals).

Gerard has successfully conducted over 5900 Trainings & Workshops (as of Sept 2022) all across India, Middle East, Africa, Europe & S.E. Asia. Besides public programs conducted regularly, both in India & Overseas, he has some of the top names as clients whom he services from Single Owners to large Public & Government undertakings, covering all sectors, for their in-house needs.

His website: www.CollectionSkills.com is the only one in this part of the world to be featured in the 'Collections & Credit Risk Magazine-USA' under 'Who's Who in Training' and ranks TOP, along with other websites listed below on most search engines.

Gerard is author of 44 books already (as on Sept 2022),
A few of the business related books being:
1. Bite-sized Bits on Commonsense Management
2. Heart to Heart on Life's Principles'
3. How to become a Successful Manager
4. The Sales Professionals' Master Workbook of S.Y.S.T.E.M.S
5. The Professional Business Email Etiquette Handbook & Guide
6. The Professional Business Video-Conferencing Etiquette Handbook & Guide
7. Professional Presentation Skills
8. Exceptional Customer Service
9. Professional Tele-Marketing Skills
10. Professional Debt Collection Skills
11. The G.R.E.A.T. Sales & Service Workbook
12. Sales Training Advantage for Results (*The Ultimate Sales Training Manual to enable you stand out as a S.T.A.R.*)
13. CEO Daily Planner & Organizer
14. The Sales Professionals' Master Daily Planner
15. The Professional Debt Collector's Master Daily Planner
16. My Daily Planner & Organizer
17. MY EMERGENCY INFORMATION RECORD (Family Emergency & Peace of Mind Planner)
18. The Ultimate Therapist & Counselors Planner and Organizer
19. Building an Ethical Workplace
20. Managing Relationships at Work
21. Managing Business Meetings Effectively

Besides regularly contributing to business & trade journals, including international ones such as the 'Creative Training Techniques' and the 'Sales News' of the U.S.A, He is also a member of several prestigious bodies & trade associations, having participated in many Conferences & Workshops in India & Overseas.

Prior to his last assignment of leading & managing a large MNC as head, Gerard had a 3-year stint in the Middle East as a Consultant with a leading British Consultancy Firm.

As the past 'Official Country Representative' for the International Business Award- 'THE STEVIES'-(the business world's own Oscar) for about 4 years- he ensured a few Indian companies that qualify for the same every year!

Gerard can be contacted at:
E: mail: training@Sales-Training.in, training@CollectionSkills.com
Websites:
www.Sales-Training.in
www.EtiquetteWorks.in
www.CollectionSkills.com
www.RetailSalesTraining.in
www.SalesTrainingIndia.com
www.ManualPreparation.com
www.TrainingWithPuppets.com
www.FirstContactAcademy.com
www.SalesAndMarketingRecruiter.com

Our TRAININGS & BOOKS that can help your team

- ✓ **Sales Effectiveness**: Selling Skills for any Sector: Service/ Logistics/ FMCG Realty/ Insurance & Finance/ Media/ SPA's, Health Clubs & Salons/ Key Account Management, Effective Negotiation Skills/ Bid & Proposal Management Skills/ Retail Sales Training: Any Sector (Auto, Jewelry, Clothing, Luxury etc)
- ✓ **Customer Service Skills**-Complaints Handling & Customer Retention
- ✓ **Debt Prevention & Collection Skills**
- ✓ **Etiquette & Grooming**
- ✓ **Leadership & Managerial Skills**
- ✓ **Self & Personal Development Skills**: Presentation Skills/ Effective Communication Skills/Business Proposal Writing Skills/ Problem Solving & Decision Making Skills/ Empowering Secretaries-The perfect PA! (For Secretaries & PA's)/ Effective Time Management/ Teamwork & Teambuilding/ P.R.I.D.E- **P**ersonal **R**esponsibility **I**n **D**elivering **E**xcellence

A Few of Our Business Books
By the Top Corporate Trainer & Author of 44 Books! (as on Sept '22)

And...DAILY PLANNERS for Every Corporate Need!

Available Online on all leading Stores

9 798215 559932